STOP WASTING TIME

Luther T. Collins

Printed in the United States of America
Published: by Legacy Voice Productions

Copyright © 2025 by Luther T. Collins

All rights reserved. This book or parts thereof may not be reproduced in any form, stored in a retrieval system, or transmitted in any form by any means- electronic, mechanical, photocopy, recording, or otherwise-without prior written permission of the author, except as provided by United States of America copyright law.

ISBN: 978-1-960179-35-7

To contact author for booking or ordering additional copies, go to:

legacyvoiceproductions@gmail.com

Table of Contents

T i m e

Life is too short

Time is nonrefundable

Investment

Make it count

One shot only

Legacy

Time

Believe it or not time is the most precious asset on earth. For it's the one thing that you can't get back. Once it's gone it's gone.

There are 24 hours in a day. While it may not seem like much time, it becomes even less when you waste the day away. It's time to ask yourself, what are you doing with your time?

How long does it take for a second to pass by? How long does it take for a minute to pass by? How long does it take for an hour to pass by? How long does it take for a day to pass by? The answer to all these questions should be not very long at all. Knowing this you have to ask yourself, what are you doing with your time?

The problem that we have as it relates with time is that we as a society are ignorant of the value time holds. Ok I get your saying this doesn't apply to me but actually it does. Just to paint a clearer picture for you, I want you to go to that place in your home where you keep your valuables. How protected are they? Are they in a safe, in a drawer, locked up, out of common vision, out of common reach, in low traffic areas?

I see your still not understanding where we are going with this. It's simple when you have something valuable you protect it and typically lock it away or take away its accessibility. Now we are going to look at it from a different lens.

Jewelry, money, gold, clothes, shoes, collectables, insurance policies, important documents, etc. can all be considered to hold a certain value. Now the question becomes what gives these items value? Uniqueness, price tag, worth, importance, usefulness, appreciation, etc. are some of the many qualities that relate to things of value.

Now let's look at time, time is unique because nothing else is like it. Time is important because it creates the moments and memories of life. Time is useful because without it you're literally not living. Time has an unlimited value because you cannot put a price tag on time. Time is important as it holds an indifferent appreciation from other things of value. When time stops so does life.

When you see the value in time you will began to appreciate its importance. Never again will you disrespect and underestimate the importance of time. Time is more

Stop Wasting Time   Luther T. Collins

than just two revolving hands that circulate around a clock.

Life is too Short

In today's world it's more important now more than ever to not let time waste away. We are living in a time where people are dying way before their time. We are living in a time where tomorrows are truly not promised.

If you need proof just look at the news. Its so many senseless killings. So many mass shootings around the world. And the number of accidental shootings and killings are steadily increasing. The wars we are fighting are becoming more intense daily.

If that wasn't enough, what about the lives covid has taken? Let's be mindful this is not the only sickness. Monkey pox, the flu, cancer, high blood pressure, diabetes, heart disease, AIDS, lupus, ectopic pregnancy, and the list goes on. These sicknesses and diseases are also responsible for taking life prematurely.

These are just some of the many examples of how one's life can end prematurely. Knowing that life is not guaranteed tomorrow and today could possibly be your last day is reason enough to make your time count. Never be so naïve that you don't believe it can happen to you.

Life is too short to waste another second, another minute, another hour, another day, another week, another month, another year, etc. It's time to live intentionally on purpose with a purpose going forward. Your legacy is your life summarized after you leave the earth. Knowing this it is imperative that you take full advantage of the time you have been given.

Stop Wasting Time			Luther T. Collins

For no individual knows the day that their time clock will end. Only God knows when that time will come.

Time is Nonrefundable

Once it's gone you can't go back. Every moment in life is an opportunity to make a memory. Ask yourself what memories will you make or what memories will you fail to make? There are no do overs, no shoulda coulda wouldas, and no rewinding the time. Since there are no refunds, you have to be mindful how you spend your time and what you choose to spend your time on.

Let me share a personal time event that took place for me where I could not get a do over. My great, great grandfather, Willie Valentine who was the matriarch and center piece of our family was always one of our first stops whenever we traveled to my hometown of Virginia after moving to North Carolina as a kid. Once we arrived in Virginia my mom said she was

Stop Wasting Time — Luther T. Collins

going to see granddaddy and I told my mom that I wanted to stay and play with my cousins so I would see him next time. The next time I saw him was at his funeral where he was in a casket.

How many people that you know share those same stories? They failed to take a moment of their time for the sake of someone else. The end result was they didn't get to say their final goodbye. Truth is it didn't hurt because he passed as he was well seasoned in age but it hurt because I passed up the opportunity to make one more memory. I missed a moment in time for a play date that would not make a memory.

It's almost like when you purchase something that you are unable to return. Maybe the store has a no return policy or maybe you missed the return window. Whichever way it goes you missed the window as that's how we are sometimes when it comes to time. We simply miss the window because we failed to make the most of our time.

With this in mind the best thing you can do is savor every moment. Never let a moment escape that has the potential to become a memory. Your time is not only precious but it's valuable. Ask yourself what value do you place on your time?

Investment

Time is truly an investment. You have both good and bad investments. When you look at the word investment, you will find that an investment is an asset that appreciates over time. This is very similar to a build up or storage for future gain.

People invest in stocks, people invest in bonds, people invest in 401k, people invest in favorable people, and people invest in asset generators. These types of investments are considered good investments. As these investments are for future preparation. The mindset behind these investments is for the financial protection and security of you, your family, and your lineage.

But watch this, people also invest in watching television, people invest in listening to music, people invest in their cell phones, and people invest in things that will not produce positive results. These types of investments are considered bad investments. This is when excessive amounts of time is spent on something that will not yield a favorable return.

This simply means if you watched television for 12 hours straight and there was no purpose, no paycheck, no deposit, and no development involved then you just wasted half of a 24 hour day. The same goes for listening to music without meaning or being on a phone without a purpose for excessive time. The negative effects of bad investments can take time off the clock for you that you can't get back.

When deciding where to invest your time you have to first understand the importance of time and then take accountability for your time. You want to be accountable for where you decide to spend your time and who you decide to spend your time with. Remember time is an investment and you can't get it back.

You can almost compare it to a timed sports game being played. It could be football, basketball, ice hockey, and the list goes on. There is a timer involved for each quarter or session of the game. When the time expires the game is over. So the athletes play as hard and skillful as they can during this time period. After the game comes to an end the players may go back and watch the replay however it will not change the outcome. Once the time expired, the buzzer sounded, the whistle was blown, etc. the allotted time officially ran out and the game ended.

This is the same with time. You invest to the best of your ability while the window is open. The one difference with life and a sporting event is you don't know when your time will expire. With this in mind you must invest in yourself and those things you spend your time on. If what you're doing is not worth the investment then it's not worth your time.

Just imagine you were to invest your life savings into something. You would definitely be mindful of what you're investing in. When you invest in something you put time, energy, and effort into a specific resource. You are simply saying that what I'm investing in is worth it with expectations that it will one day yield a favorable return.

Make It Count

Now knowing everything that has been shared so far about time, you should now see that you have to make it count. Making it count is simply not letting an opportunity escape to turn a moment into a memory. This is the attitude of gratitude we must have as it relates to time.

Let's think about those who go to the doctor and get a bad report. Maybe they have been diagnosed with cancer and only given 6 months to live. They have two options: they can cry over it or they can simply make each moment count. Knowing the situation and that there is nothing you can do to change it, do you really want to spend your last days crying, complaining, or in depression? Or do you want to enjoy your family one last time with one last laugh, one last smile, one last cry of joy, etc.?

Let's go back to the person who has been given a bad report but let's make it personal. If it was your mom, your dad, your sister, your brother, your spouse, your child, your loved one, etc. how would you respond? When you look at it from a personal perspective it changes your outlook. Your new view is one of making it count especially knowing that time is nonrefundable and there is no reimbursement plan.

A timeline is not always one of depression, so let's look at it from another angle. For the purpose of painting a picture, let's say you don't have any transportation. Let's say you decide to lease a car for a year or even rent a car for a month. During this time is when you would maximize having a vehicle. Especially since you have to pay (invest) for this vehicle in order to rent or lease it.

Now knowing what you know about time it is everyone's responsibility to make it count. Going forward don't let time escape your presence without making every moment count. Stop letting time leave your presence without reaping an investment, make it count.

Only One Shot

Remember we only got one shot at this thing called life. And our life consists of the time from our birth to our death. Steve Harvey said it best, "You will only be remembered by the dash on your tombstone!" This simply says that your sunrise to your sunset is your summary.

Let's go back to the sports example that we talked about a little earlier. If we take a basketball game with 3 seconds left on the shot clock to determine the game outcome, strategy must come into place. First you must determine who will shoot the final shot to win the game. Will it be Michael Jordan? Will it be Steph Curry? Will it be LeBron James? The coach draws the play and maybe determines LeBron will pass it to Steph Curry who comes off a screen that MJ sets for the game winner.

If we are talking football, maybe its 7 seconds left on the game clock in the super bowl with a tied game. Maybe the New York Giants have the ball on the New England Patriots 20 yard line. The coach must decide whether we are going to kick a field goal or are we going to try to get into the end zone. Let's say the kicker got hurt, now what do you do? Strategy must come into play where the coach only has one shot to help his team get the W.

If we are talking ice hockey and its 10 seconds on the clock as the game is tied 1 to 1. We have to decide who will take the game winning shot. Who will make the pass to get the game winning shot? Again the coach must take a time out to determine what play will be run and who will be the key players as well as who will be the decoys.

As given with each example each team had to create a strategy and game plan. The outcome of the game would be determined based on the play they call or fail to call. They could be considered champions or they could be runner ups based on what they do with the allotted time given.

When we tie this into life it renders the same verdict based on the decisions you make as it relates to time. Will you be considered a champion of time or a failure because you failed to make the most of the time you were given?

Legacy

You're probably wondering, how does time tie into legacy? What does legacy have to do with time? Believe it or not, legacy has everything to do with time. Your legacy is a reflection of your time here on earth.

How you spend your time and where you spend your time all equals legacy. Legacy is not just what you leave behind but what you build while you're here. You will only be remembered by what you did while you were living.

The question on the table is what will your legacy of time reflect? Will it reflect that you were wasteful or watchful? Will it reflect that you made the most of each moment or that you let moments pass you by? Ask yourself what memories have you made and what memories have you missed?

Answer these questions truthfully and honestly as it will only assist you to get on track to ensure your time builds your legacy. Be watchful of how you spend your time and what you do with your time. Be careful of what you invest your time in. If it does not have the potential to produce a favorable outcome it may not be worth your time.

Never let moments escape that have the potential to produce memories. Life has so many precious events, that's why we take pictures, that's why we record audio and video, that's why we develop pictures and create photo albums, and so on. What moments and memories do you hold close to your heart?

The baby's very first step, the wedding day, the anniversary, the baptism date, the graduation date, the funeral, the birth, the birthday, the promotion, the production, the premiere, and so many more. These are all precious moments that turned into lasting memories. It's the lasting memories of these moments that create legacy.

Your time is worth the investment. Your investment is worth the time. Life does not come with a replay, rewind, recital, or reverse. It is up to you to determine how your time will be spent and what legacy your time will leave behind.

Leaving
Everlasting
Greatness
Allowing
Celebrations
Year round

This is what legacy maximization looks like as it relates to time. You leave behind treasures for the future generation to find. You understand that while your life will one day end you can plant everlasting seeds for the next generations. Your greatness is deposited in the soil of the earth. You allow your time to be maximized. You celebrate every moment and every memory. Year round you take advantage of the commodity of time.

Time and legacy go hand and hand like a husband and wife. Always remember this, "Your time here on earth is your legacy. And your legacy is a reflection of your time here on earth."

After reading this book do you believe that time is the most precious treasure on earth and why or why not?

_____
_____
_____
_____
_____
_____
_____

What legacy will you leave behind for your future generations?

_____
_____
_____
_____
_____
_____
_____

What moments and memories will you be intentional about creating going forward?

_____
_____
_____
_____
_____
_____
_____

What will you do to going forward to make the most of your time?

_____
_____
_____
_____
_____
_____
_____

What are you willing to invest to ensure your legacy produces a favorable outcome?

_____
_____
_____
_____
_____
_____
_____

How will you make your days count going forward?

_____
_____
_____
_____
_____
_____
_____

www.ingramcontent.com/pod-product-compliance
Lightning Source LLC
Chambersburg PA
CBHW071804040426
42446CB00012B/2709